This book is dedicated to my readers, my parents and 'Feminist'.

# SCRIBBLINGS IN “QUARTER LIFE CRISIS”

RANDOM SCRIBBLINGS

ADWAIT VATS

# Contents

# Contents

# Contents

# Deserted Verge

Long before I met myself on a deserted verge, I had started noticing the lonely souls walking around with naked emotions. And I wondered why everyone kept their distance from them. Was it because they were so exposed and whoever took an abrupt glimpse couldn't help from averting their eyes, or was it because they saw their own vulnerable reflection in them? Now I know when I am one of them: sometimes the spectator and sometimes the spectacle.

# Oh! Paramour

Smitten by hitherto beats of your charming heart,
engulfed like a tambourine, erasing all my agony like a
fading moonlight, I burn the stains of despair. I cure my
carmine lacerated skin, with lien that waved beads of your
vigor. Oh! Paramour, without you I'm enervated.
Drowning in the vale of undying love, I stay alive
reciprocating your breath.

# She Says...

Define me beyond my own depths she says. Imagine me beyond your worst impulses she urges. But, by no assertive means ever scheme to cease my flight she warns.

For my fearless wings, don't bow to your cynical forces.

# Love Again

I am absolutely incapable of loving a single person. The way I see it, I am not a single person myself. I'm many. I'm lots of people in a single body. I'm scattered across different minds, like the stardust that is floating through the space. You can't contain me. You can't make me whole. So then, how do you expect me to believe in a single love? My love is not whole. My love is flawed. My love is divine but not defined. So, let it all come and consume me because I have dared myself to love again.

# Heavenly like an Angel

She looked like a heaven in daylight, smelt like the petrichor of the countryside. She wore a rainbow for a smile, so colourful like the autumn leaves. She left footprints of bliss in my heart, spreading beauty like a shooting star.

She sounded heavenly like an angel singing hallelujah, butterflies blossomed from the sound of her voice.

# My Love

My love for you has grown roots deep inside me, if you ever choose to walk away, know that you'll rip out my heart.

Strong, robust tentacles of foundation inside my chest growing and growing.

A plant too energized for my lethargic body. A plant that provides me the ability to breathe, A plant that takes away my ability to breathe. I can't wait till it turns into a tree.

We'll build a treehouse in the branches, won't we?

# Forever Flaw

You're like a jagged edge on my smooth surface. A scratch on the vinyl where the needle keeps getting caught. The crack through the middle of a mirror, a reflection of true imperfection. You're my forever flaw that identifies my true character.

# Interdigitated

They both lived in different worlds. He had a magic carpet. She had a field of wildflowers. In his carpet, he would roam around his world and capture the dancing waves. And in her world, she would run free among the wildflowers and tell them her darkest secrets. Not often did their worlds collide. But when it did, they would see the wildflowers dancing in the middle of the sea. When it did, everything else would seem unreal. When it did, nothing else would make sense, not even love.

# Home

Some people are like home. Like a safe space where you can hide yourself in the rainstorm. They would see that you are shivering from the cold and put a blanket over your shoulders. Sometimes, you would have to make that warm soup for yourself but they would show you where the ingredients are. And if you are afraid of the thunder, they might even tuck you in their arms. The next day when the storm passes, you might leave each other, because you are a wanderer, and you've got places to go. But as you leave, you always know in your heart that you've a home in the mountains, where you are always welcome.

# I'm making tea for us

"You talk so much about love without getting tired of it, even your saddest poems are gentle. I’ve seen you talking to someone in the lines, but never saw you sending those letters, Do they know you? Are you in love with-"

"Look at the sky, how pretty it looks. Come in, I'm making tea for us."

# I'm not here to climb

There was a mountain that stood majestically before her. She would tell her friends that one day she would climb up to its top. It didn't take long for her to start the journey. But every day, she only moved little by little, stopping now and then to see something that amused her. Seeing this, a fellow traveler told her, " You seem to be out of focus. At this rate, you'll never make it to the top." She looked at the traveler and grinned mischievously. The traveler was fascinated by the excitement in her eyes. She came closer and said softly into his ears, "Don't tell anyone, I'm not here for the climb. I'm here to listen to what the wind whispers to the mountain, in secret."

# I'm not here to [illegible]

There was a [illegible] She would [illegible] up to its top. It didn't [illegible] But every day, she [illegible] and then to see [illegible] fellow traveler [illegible] this rate, you'll [illegible]

traveler and [illegible] fascinated by [illegible] and said soft[illegible] here for the [illegible] wh[illegible]

# life within yourself

It all happened when your chaos was fast asleep. For years they told you to suppress it. With your weary eyes you saw it dozing off, whenever something troubled your soul. "It's safer this way", they told you. And you kept quiet, whenever you wanted to spit fire one the beasts that fed on your demons. "Chaos is the weapon of a monster", they warned you. And you hid away your turmoil whenever it knocked on your door, in fear of becoming a monster. Today I tell you that they were lying; they were frightened of your blazing soul that transforms chaos into beauty. Today I tell you to unleash your chaos, cuddle up with your madness, embrace the havoc and nurture it like a newborn, until you find life within yourself.

# Fall even harder

.... And without doubt he fell for her each time she placed a broken piece of heart into his shattered core. He had convinced himself that it was never meant to be whole again, but she was a moonlight girl who danced with his demons; the wildflower who ushered her roots to mend his scars. Now and then he would peep into her soul and feel the tremors, and with each quiver he would fall even harder for the way she was herself, all the time.

# No Shivers

The tears on her cheeks were the only warmth she felt. When it dried up, the cold crawled in and numbed her nerves. She waited until she felt nothing; until all her emotions faded; until life walked out from her soul. She waited until the cold didn't bother her anymore. And when people saw her turn cold, she no longer felt the shivers.

# Surprise

Greatest surprise is the one you gave to yourself. Sometimes you do things and wonder, "How the hell did I do it", Sometimes you overcome a situation that had drained you and think, " I thought I will never make through it", Sometimes you seem to become a person you never knew you were. We surprise overselves often, cause deep inside there is still a 'You', yet to be discovered.

# It was different for Him

She loved him because he was a sad poem. She would run her fingers through his broken words and cover herself with grief. She would say it made her alive. It made her feel deep. But it was different for him. The least he could do was hide her in her poems and hope that someday when she read it aloud, the words would whisper her name.

# Emptiness

He fell asleep by the window seat, the gentle breeze fondling his wild hair.

Stirred by her warm breath he opened his eyes in half hesitation, only to find an empty seat beside. Remnants of some broken memories jerked out from the graveyard of past and grinned at his brutally. His eyes fixed far-off, a sigh of emptiness.

# Friend Asked

One day my friend asked me, "why people fail to understand each other sometimes?" I took out my lighter, lit it, grabbed his finger and placed over it, "Does it hurt?", "Damn! my finger! Are you nuts?". "I understand that you're hurt, but the intensity of your pain, only you know".

# Afraid to Love?

To those who are afraid of love, I understand you. I know that fear of love can be the worst of fears. I know that it's terrifying when the only thing you thought would heal your crushes you to nothingness. And I know that it will be hard for you to listen to me, but I want you to save your soul; through love. Let's start by loving ourselves. And one day, I promise you, it will feel right, and then nothing else would matter.

# Are they free?

He was lying on his bed thinking about thoughts. Are they free? They came in and out so carefree. He watched them fill his mind like how air filled his lungs. His soul expanded, and he took a deep and relaxing breath. So, are they free? Do I decide when to breathe and when not? Do I decide what to think and what not? Thoughts, let them come in and out like the air, free and wild. But then he heard someone gasping for air. What happened? Who is blocking the air? Was it not free? He felt himself shrinking. His thoughts choked and died, left out to rot. Now, he lay there with an empty stare, thinking about those who died choking.

# Deceive

Long long ago I had an affinity to sadness; which wrapped me firmly, like a mad lover holding his beloved. Happiness always stood there, smiling; never did I dared to look, never did I turned around. But today, I am here to deceive sadness; by mistake, I have fallen in love with happiness.

# She's a Wildflower

She is a wildflower that grows in you like madness. No wonder that you fell for her arresting wildness; her roots that heaved strength from the neglected wilderness, taught her to spit fire out of her petals. Sway your gaze, O ravaging mortals! Touch her, and you will see her arising from your ashes. No, do not call her a phoenix; she's a wildflower.

# Who will save all those sinking souls?

I don't promise to save all the sinking souls. Not even once it occurred to me to grow their hands; let the sea elope them, I was there only to watch the sunset. But as the sun faded and the darkness expanded my horizon, a brutal pain grew in my bosom; and I knew I couldn't let them down. I fought the violent waves and made my way to the calling of the sinking souls; I clutched my soul to their finger tips and let myself become their last hope. I pulled at once, but sank more. I kept pulling till I drowned and hit the bottom. And now I worry, who will save all those sinking souls?

# He darns his wound

He sucked into his veins everything that tasted like fire. Now it the sky couldn't stand his fervour you can't blame him; He darns his wounds with the flames that burn him.

# Piece of You

Today I found a little piece of you left in me. I locked it away in the depths of my core and threw away the key. I hope I never find it. But I hope, if I ever found it, I would open the safe gently and look at it like the way I used to look at your starry eyes. I hope I get drunk by your scent and forget the pain of my existence. And I hope I let it go. let you go. But what if my yearnings tear me apart? What if they still want to know how your lips blended with mine?

# Stalwart

Somnolent silence is the solemn sanctity. Where the splintered soul get mends to a stalwart.

# I Scribble

I scribble. I pen down. I scratch my pen on a sheet of paper. Unconsciously, I describe your presence.

Aren't you the one, pacing in my imaginations?*

# Mummy-Papa

When merely the hollowness embraces me, the only light that fills my heart. Whenever this cruel earth breaks me, the only hope to collect my shattered pieces and move on.

I open my little arms wide, pout my mouth, whine like a puppy and snuggle into them with squeals "Mummy, Papa",

In their warmth, I always feel like I'm a toddler for them.

# Ignorance

"What's my first thought when I had finished high school?"
Mind asked.

"You need not to study hard as much as you did before."
Emotions replied.

Ignorance creepily smiles from corner of my heart.

# Walk Away

My silhouette is shifting to the north pole of loneliness again, ice cold and forlorn. Far from this temporary bliss, bearing in mind the inevitable truth- eternity is a cruel hoax.

But, you've been here for a while with open arms and steady eyes. So, I ask with the last ray of hope in my heart...Will you leave me in December as you did in May? Or is it really time for one of us to walk away?

# Circular Tea Stains

If I were a memory, I would be those circular tea stains imprinted on a table long left unattended— stuck, waiting for someone to pull out a dirty rug and rub me off. I'll be there the next day.

# Beautiful Lie

I left my soul in my diary, with some endless orphic phrases of my life. Now, I'm just a solivagent, fragile piece of flesh, searching for an another beautiful lie.

# I Abandon You

I abandon. I vandalise all that is left of you in me. Erase your touch, sabotage your cologne, and remove a pair from the trail if footprints.

But, this isn't destruction. It's an art made out of one.

It's how I choose to abandon you.

# Poets Say

She is made of magic, stardust and memories. A free soul that belongs to a wanderer in the wilderness and beauty oblivious to time like the poets say.

# Wore Her Scars

She wore her scars like stars, Hymn the song of storm.
Telling the world, she isn't afraid of judgements. I, here,
belong.

# Your Eyes

For you the heavens wouldn't suffice, and for me the heaven shines in your eyes.

# To Continue Her Journey

Her old feathers were heavy, torn apart and kept her on the ground; She had to pluck them out even though it was painful. She waited for her new feathers to fully grow, to be strong, to be beautiful; then walked to the highest edge to stretch her wings and to continue her journey which she once kept aside.

# Let Poets Suffer

We let poets suffer in silence blooming emotions; We let them stay inside maternity wards of their minds conceiving poetries and nourishing verses when solitude impregnates.

# She Wanders

She wanders those broken paths, where moon floats and hides behind Reims; betwixt hope and hell, she carries on.

# Sleep

That sleep, is not anymore, the same.

I need to sleep to have a side life,

A side life to escape from reality.

A reality that's way more rough.

The roughness which is more like a call out.

A call out with a whirl of gloom.

The gloom that hinges on me for ever.

Because for ever, it's just that sleep which would keep me in the frame.

# Sand Castle

I build my sand castle and then it rains. But, that's alright I just build it again.

I get tripped up sometimes by the pain.

Distracted and temporarily lose my place.

I've created a life line with my imagination.

It helps me to paint a better picture.

Of who I am versus who I wasn't, A man hardened by all his problems.

The magic in nature holds my hand, showing me new ways to understand.

I'm becoming something I never thought I could be, dancing over the top of the trees. Everything is like a dream come true, everything including you.

# Nihilism

Nihilism made me hollow.

Before, empathy kept flooding me.

I was preserving to be detached, now, I cannot feel any.

I was only searching for some absolution.

But then, only death is absolute. So, I have practiced to die.

I have practiced to live, Now I can't tell which is what
crawling inside.

# I know Her

I know her when she's broken. I know her when she's taken. I'm her mirror after all I reflect her flaws and accept her flawsomeness unlike the world that pushes her to fake a flawless life...!!

# Dictated Hope

In a pit of hole, I dictated hope.

I'm a bigot living as a bohemian. An altruist you can call.

Devastated. Destructed. Life piling up stocks affected. Let's sit and talk of iconoclast. Impregnable. Impostor.

At times narcissistic. At times introvert. Let's cross lands, rivers and aisles. Let's share concoction of stories. Connect and grow. Live life of one another!

# Electronic Lantern

The electronic lantern is lighting my face to kick-start the
poetic phase of the night.

The lantern is my mobile that handles my hurricane of
thoughts to strain the strains and pains of the day and
present the aesthetic sediments as my poetry.

# Optimistic Incarcerated

Resonating incessant pain. Painting my persona as a pessimist. But, my hidden optimistic incarcerated in me, helps me to bear the deafening gossips.

# Home in my Soul

The pain in your heart found its home in my soul. Flustered, my heart started to do its job as always. To cure everyone's pain expecting nothing in return.

# Dark Sky

Talk to me through your eyes and I'll tell you why stars
look beautiful only on dark sky.

# My Heart was a Wreck

My heart was a wreck but in you I found someone who loved my ruins.

# Saga of your Love

You, the cure of my timorous heart. your emollient smile,
tethers my soul. Words, slithering me whole.

As I seize my eyes, burthens lie in peace. I'm lost betwixt
the saga of your love and the erroneous expectations.

# Soul's Sync

The melody of your words, accompanied by the
embodiment of doting, is a bliss, indeed!

The repeating sounds unearth the truth of wanting you.

Taste of passion between us debates, as our souls' sync.

# I vie for togetherness

I vie for togetherness, I let your love seep deep and engulf my life with serenity. The cacophony of chaos doesn't bother me anymore as we saunter.

## Sempiternal

Exhaling vehemence in my heart, I read my love filled lines. Until they take me closer to you. I purloin the skies as well as romantic hues just for you.

# Gush of wanting You

Your eyes, filled with souvenirs of cluttered feelings and a canopy of unsatisfied metaphors. Increases the gush of wanting you, I lure for the claustrophobic release with bated breath.

9 798887 491462

Printed by Libri Plureos GmbH in Hamburg,
Germany